THE SECOND WORLD WAR

Teacher's resource book

With photocopy masters

Sean Lang
Head of History
Hills Road Sixth Form College,
Cambridge

Published by the Press Syndicate of the University of Cambridge
The Pitt Building, Trumpington Street, Cambridge CB2 1RP
40 West 20th Street, New York, NY 10011 – 4211, USA
10 Stamford Road, Oakleigh, Melbourne 3166, Australia

© Cambridge University Press 1993

First published 1993

A catalogue record for this book is available from the British Library.

ISBN 0 521 43827 6 paperback

Produced by Gecko Limited, Bicester, Oxon

Printed in Great Britain at the University Press, Cambridge

Every effort has been made to reach copyright holders. The
publishers would be pleased to hear from anyone whose rights
they have unwittingly infringed.

Contents

Photocopiable resource sheets

A Appeasement (Unit 2)

A map and a chart with relevant data enable pupils to give informed advice to Chamberlain on the feasibility of appeasing Hitler.

B Civil defence (Units 4 and 5)

Pupils are given the task of organising an air raid drill for their school. By using their modern-day schools and then making allowances for conditions in 1940 pupils get an idea of the scale of the problems facing ordinary people during the war and, by extension, of the problems facing their leaders.

C–D The Battle of Britain (Unit 4)

A diagram shows how the British system of air defence worked, including Radar and Observers. Pupils examine the system carefully for weak links and come up with plans either to exploit them or plug them. By comparing their plans with the actual plans that were followed in the battle, pupils get a clearer understanding of the reasons for the German defeat.

E The King of Denmark and the Star of David?

Against the background of Nazi anti-semitism, the pupils consider the problem of establishing the authenticity of sources. This popular story had wide currency in Denmark and elsewhere both during and after the war. How can we establish whether it is true or apocryphal? Even if this is not possible, what can we learn from the widespread circulation and acceptance of such stories and their eventual questioning by historians?

F–G The Russian Front (Unit 7)

These resource sheets allow pupils to analyse the events of the war in Russia and, by using a timeline, place them in chronological order while also deciding which side benefited from the outcome.

H Pearl Harbor (Unit 8)

While the text in the pupils' book concentrates on the reasons for the Japanese attack, here the pupils are invited to consider its consequences. This involves looking ahead from 1941 in order to assess the significance of the attack. The same sort of exercise can, of course, be applied to other events during the war.

I The Holocaust (Unit 9)

Pupils take on the role of lawyers involved in the Nazi war crimes trials, researching and presenting evidence of Nazi attitudes towards and then treatment of the Jews.

J Code breaking

There is at least a strong case (some would say unanswerable) for attributing Allied success in the war to the work of the code breakers, who cracked the Japanese MAGIC and the German ENIGMA coding systems early on in the war. This exercise in logic and map reading gives pupils just a little idea of this work – the more so since it has to be completed against the clock! This exercise is not designed to fit into any specific unit, though it is of relevance to the sections on defence against bombing, and to the story of the Battle of the Atlantic. The base lies slightly to the north of Amiens. The towns are Sheffield (Schmalstigel), Bristol (Bruder), Southampton (Suden) and Birmingham (Bild).

K–L Propaganda (Unit 5 and 6)

This is of relevance to a wide selection of aspects of the war. Taking Goebbels' famous guidelines for propaganda as their starting point, pupils are invited to create their own versions of propaganda, relating it to a variety of different events. They also look at the illustrations in books as a form of propaganda. This can easily lead to discussion of the merits of various forms of presentation both of current events and of the past.

M 'Funny' tanks (Unit 11)

The popular image of D-Day is of an invincible build-up of strength. In fact the Allied planners had numerous problems to cope with, some of which called for ingenious solutions. In this exercise pupils match tank designs with the sort of obstacles that tanks would have met on the Normandy beachhead. The 'deep water' tank is D, the 'boggy ground' one is B, the 'ditch' one is E and the 'minefield' one is C. They then produce a further tank design to overcome another problem they envisage could also have been encountered on D-Day. Having worked on these problems, pupils will be in a better position to appreciate the solutions that the Allied planners did actually come up with in 1944.

N–O The Liberation of Paris (Unit 12)

General von Choltitz was the man charged by Hitler with either defending Paris to the death or destroying it completely. This 'in-tray' exercise puts pupils in the role of advisers to the General, with an eye both to the advancing Allies and to the watchful SS.

P–Q Is Hitler dead? (Unit 12)

Recurrent stories of sightings of Hitler continued to hit the press for thirty years after the end of the war. This unit looks at the evidence for what happened to Hitler, including the various pieces of disinformation issued by Moscow. It also gives rise to discussion about the continuing fascination the Third Reich holds for many people. The issue of the fake Hitler diaries bought in 1982 by the German magazine *Stern* and serialised in *The Sunday Times* could also be raised in this connection.

R Dropping the bomb (Unit 13)

The controversy surrounding the decision to drop the atomic bombs on Hiroshima and Nagasaki continues today. This unit looks at the various factors affecting the American decision to drop the bomb. In the role of advisers to the President, pupils must decide, considering all the factors, what the decision should be.

S War crimes (Unit 14)

The Nuremberg Trial has often been attacked as 'victors' justice', and even in 1946 there was concern on the Allied side that this was so in the case of the German naval leaders put on trial. Pupils are presented with a section of the cross-examination of Admiral Doenitz and invited to consider whether or not unrestricted submarine warfare counts as a war crime. There are obvious links to earlier units and exercises, including the issue of similar tactics being used on the Allied side, but this can also be used to link up with more recent atrocities in South East Asia, the Middle East and former Yugoslavia.

T The Truman Doctrine and Marshall Aid (Units 14 and 15)

Czechoslovakia, before it fell to Soviet power, was keen to sign up for American Marshall Aid. The Russians were keen to prevent this. Pupils look at the conflicting claims about Marshall Aid and prepare a party political broadcast to argue the case for or against acceptance. This gives a useful introduction to the issue of economic dominance and the post-war 'informal empires' of the two super-powers.

U End of empire

The end of the war brought the mighty European empires crashing down very shortly afterwards. What part did the war play in this? This exercise in causes and consequences invites pupils to use their knowledge in order to estimate the role the war played in weakening European authority in Asia and Africa.

V–W The war remembered

No one, least of all children, can escape from the Second World War. In films, memorials, books, even in toys, its influence is all-pervasive. Pupils consider the image of the war presented in a variety of forms of popular culture, and consider the thorny question of the presentation of the Holocaust.

The pupils' book is divided into three main sections, each introduced by an overview of the topics to be studied. It simply is not possible at this level to look in detail at all aspects of such a complicated topic.

These notes will help teachers to put some elements of the text into a wider context. Books suitable for children are marked with an asterisk(*).

Total war (Introduction)
Democracy and dictatorship (Unit 1)
Two decades of aggression (Overview)

These sections are designed to give an idea of the scale of the conflict. Geographically, there was hardly an area of the globe that was not affected, in most cases directly. Almost every human activity imaginable, from baking a cake to theoretical physics, was harnessed to the war effort.

Unit 1 looks at the ideologies that were in conflict in the 1920s and 1930s, which came to a head in the war. The overview section *Two decades of aggression* gives an idea of the context in which these issues came to blows. This will be familiar territory to many teachers from GCSE, and indeed some pupils might be encouraged to supplement their reading with GCSE texts.

Pupils might ponder the fact that the democracies lined up during the war with Stalin's dictatorship. A massive propaganda campaign in Britain and America strove to present Stalinism in the most favourable light possible. As well as posters and a grand 'Salute to the Soviet Union' held in the Albert Hall, a special ornate sword was presented by George VI to Stalin in honour of the defence of Stalingrad. So effective was this blurring of the distinctions between democracy and dictatorship that the first post-war reports of Soviet espionage activity in the West were not at first believed.

Pupils might be encouraged to consider the implications of wartime alliances of expediency: they should also be reminded that from August 1939 (the Nazi–Soviet Pact) until Operation Barbarossa in 1941 Germany and the Soviet Union were allies, and shared in the carving up of Poland.

Useful reading:
A useful recent treatment of the two major dictators of this period is Alan Bullock's *Hitler and Stalin: Parallel Lives* (Harper Collins), while A.J.P. Taylor's *The War Lords* (Penguin) gives short thumbnail sketches of all the major war leaders.

Germany prepares for war (Unit 2)
Blitzkrieg (Unit 3)
Britain embattled (Unit 4)

The normal picture of the German blitzkrieg given in books and documentaries is of an invincible force driving through its victims like a knife through butter. Although this will do for the overall effect, there were a number of important local differences from this general image. The Poles, for example, did possess tanks as well as cavalry and in open country cavalry could still be very effective, as the Russians were to show later in the war. Moreover, the German army relied very heavily on horsepower throughout the war, though for transport rather than for battle. Similarly, although the Germans reached Warsaw quickly, the Polish resistance in the capital was much fiercer than they had expected, and only collapsed when the Russians attacked in the east.

There is a similar problem with the usual picture of events in the west. The Germans ran into severe problems in Holland, where the Dutch proved tough fighters, and German paratroop drops to seize the Dutch bridges came close to disaster. The bombing of Rotterdam is still the subject of controversy: it seems likely that much of the damage resulted from a margarine factory that caught fire. Similarly, it would be wrong to let the pupils think that the Germans encountered no strong resistance from the British and French. In the end it was the Germans' superior tactics that defeated the Allies. The effects of French defeatism have, it now seems clear, been greatly exaggerated, at least for the period up until the final surrender: thereafter the humiliation of defeat, coupled with the British destruction of the French fleet at Oran and Mers-el-Kebir, quickly turned French opinion against their erstwhile allies.

The campaigns in Unit 4 are fairly well known. It is worth underlining for pupils what a close thing the Battle of Britain was, and even more so for the Battle of the Atlantic. The North African campaign was never much more than a sideshow in terms of the war as a whole, though it diverted valuable German troops from the Russian campaign, and was at the time the only way the British could get their army into contact with the Germans.

Useful reading:
Len Deighton's *Blitzkrieg* (Cape) and *Fighter* (Cape) give excellent overall views of the campaigns of 1940; Alistair Horne's *To Lose a Battle: France 1940* (Penguin) gives a

good idea of what went wrong on the French side; *The Last Enemy* (Pan) is Richard Hillary's moving account of his experiences in the Battle of Britain; Martin Middlebrook's *Convoy* (Penguin) and Nicholas Monserrat's *The Cruel Sea* (Penguin) both give vivid pictures of the desperate convoy battles in the north Atlantic, the latter in fictional form;

Spike Milligan's *Adolf Hitler: My Part in his Downfall* (Penguin) gives a funny and moving account of his time in the western desert, and pupils might also look at the poetry the war produced, in collections like *Poems of the Second World War** (Nelson/Oasis).

The Home Front in Britain (Unit 5)
Life under Hitler (Unit 6)

There is scope here for pupils to talk with older people who remember the war to amplify the account they have in the pupils' book. In particular, it is worth looking into the question of just how accurate the generally optimistic picture of the 'Spirit of the Blitz' really is. Although it reflects the overall effect, there were a number of important local exceptions to this general pattern.

Much the same might be asked of the general picture of life in occupied Europe. The old picture, in which every other citizen was active in the Resistance, has long been questioned, and the extent of collaboration is a lot clearer now than it used to be. The Holocaust is treated in a separate unit, but pupils should consider how they would react to the perpetrators of, say, Lidice. Equally, it is worth pointing out that, as long as you were not of the wrong race or creed, life in Nazi Germany could be pleasant: if not, it would hardly be possible to explain popular support for Hitler.

Useful reading:
Perhaps the best known account of life in Nazi Germany is Christabel Bielenberg's *The Past is Myself* (Corgi). Ian Serraillier's *The Silver Sword** (Puffin) gives a good picture of life in occupied Poland, and has the added merit of being written for children. On the home front in Britain, there are plenty of materials aimed at GCSE students. Caroline Lang has produced a valuable look at women in the war in *Keep Smiling Through** (CUP). *The Machine Gunners** by Robert Westall (Macmillan) is a well-known account of life on the Home Front seen through children's eyes in the North East, while David Rees' *The Exeter Blitz** (Heinemann) shows a child living through the Baedekker Raids in the South West. For a good account of evacuation, see *Carrie's War** by Nina Bawden, (Gollancz) while *And the Policeman Smiled* by Barry Turner (Bloomsbury) gives a good picture of evacuation of a different kind: to England from Nazi Germany.

The Russian Front (Unit 7)

Very few western books give enough emphasis to the Russian Front. Its scale was so vast that it virtually dwarfed almost any other front. The account here has inevitably had to telescope the events, leaving out the massive tank battle of Kursk in 1943, the largest tank battle ever fought. The most striking aspect of the Russian campaign is its bitterness: German soldiers dreaded being sent to it. The agony of the Siege of Leningrad can hardly be overstressed.

Useful reading:
There is a good account of the opening phase on the

Russian Front in Nikolai Tolstoy's *Victims of Yalta* (Corgi), though the main emphasis of the book is on the fate of the White Russians and Cossacks handed back to Stalin after the war. Harrison Salisbury's *The Siege of Leningrad** (Penguin) gives a full and harrowing account of what it was like to live through the worst siege in history. For a young German's experiences on this front, see *The Time of the Young Soldiers** by Hans Peter Richter (Armada). Stalin's purges, that left the Soviet Union so unprepared in 1941, are described in Robert Conquest's *The Great Terror* (Macmillan).

War in the east (Overview)
Pearl Harbor (Unit 8)

The soldiers fighting in Burma used to complain that they were the 'Forgotten Army', and much the same sort of problem tends to pervade most treatment of the war in Asia. It is easy to forget that the fighting in Burma and on the Pacific islands was going on right up until the last day of the war.

The western soldiers built up an image of their Japanese enemies as invincible and cunning, which still makes it difficult for us to see the Japanese of that period as human

beings. The inhuman treatment meted out in Japanese prison camps, which included 'medical' experiments similar to those carried out in Nazi concentration camps, still colours western views of wartime Japan. Less well known are the appalling cruelties carried out by Japanese troops against the native populations they conquered. More Philippine and Burmese civilians died in Japanese labour camps than Allied personnel. In China, Japanese troops were responsible for widespread cruelty, including mass rapes carried out in Shanghai. These events still sour relations between Japan and China today. It is perhaps worthth pointing out to pupils that in 1991, on the fiftieth anniversary of Pearl Harbor, President Bush was still unable to wring a word of apology out of Japan for the attack, and Japanese schools still do not teach about the atrocities committed by Japanese troops during the war.

Useful reading:
Pierre Boulle's *Bridge on the River Kwai* and J.G. Ballard's *Empire of the Sun* (Gollancz), both the subject of successful films, give an idea of what life was like under Japanese guard. Two volumes in Longman's *Modern Times* Sourcebook series give a selection of useful source material on the two combattants in the Pacific: *Japan 1850–1985** by Stuart Fewster (Longman) and *America 1870–1975** by John O'Keeffe (Longman).

The Holocaust (Unit 9)

Teachers need to approach this topic with great care. There is a vast literature about the pitfalls involved in teaching about the Holocaust. While there is general agreement that it is important to teach children about what happened, there is a danger of presenting a stereotyped picture that causes even more offence. In particular, while it is obvious that the Jews and the others sent to the camps were very much victims, nevertheless there were a number of important incidents of resistance, notably the Warsaw Ghetto rising and an attempted mass break-out from Sobibor that forced the Germans to destroy the camp. Similarly, while Jews were by far the largest group of inmates, there were plenty of others. Gypsies, homosexuals, trade unionists and political opponents of the Nazis, captured resistance fighters and others who were deemed by the Nazis to have defied German rule, were all sent to the camps. The plight of Russian prisoners of war is worth stressing, for they were deliberately starved and worked to death, and those who were released were either massacred by Stalin's secret police or sent to his own concentration camps.

Useful reading:
Far and away the best known piece of writing on the Holocaust is the *Diary of Anne Frank** (Pan), though inevitably it cannot give a picture of life in the camps. *When Hitler Stole Pink Rabbit** by Judith Kerr (Collins) gives another child's-eye view, covering both Nazi Germany and her escape to England. *From Prejudice to Genocide* by Carrie Supple (Trentham) is an excellent teachers' resource, with material on a wide variety of aspects of the Holocaust, including eyewitness testimony from concentration camp survivors. *Carve her Name with Pride** by R.J. Minney (Armada) tells the story of the SOE agent Violette Szabo, and includes an account of her last days in Ravensbruck. The Imperial War Museum publishes a valuable collection of eyewitness accounts in *The Relief of Belsen, 1945* (Imperial War Museum). There is a brief but vivid glimpse of the plight of Russian POWs in Eric Williams' escape drama *The Wooden Horse** (Armada).

Bombing (Unit 10)
Allied conferences (Overview)
D-Day (Unit 11)
Germany collapses (Unit 12)

The Allied bombing campaign still arouses strong emotions, as witness the controversy over the statue of Sir Arthur Harris erected in 1992. Pupils will certainly need to confront the issue, though as always it is important to avoid shallow or facile judgements. Argument tends to centre on the Dresden raid of February 1945. There is some dispute as to who was actually responsible for the raid: Churchill tried to back off shortly after it and to shift the blame onto Harris, though it seems clear that Harris was merely attacking the target he was told to. There is also controversy about the casualty figures at Dresden: the usual quoted figure is 60,000 but this is almost certainly far too high, and the true figure may be nearer 20,000. There is a full discussion of the figures in D. Saward's *Bomber Harris* cited in the text. It is perhaps worth noting that Canon Collins, the Bomber Command chaplain who first voiced criticism of the

campaign, went on to become a leading figure in CND.

The Overview on Allied conferences is an attempt to put otherwise rather dry affairs into a form readily accessible to children. The speech bubbles are not quotations, but they do represent the positions of the various leaders at the conferences.

D-Day, like Dunkirk and the Blitz, has developed a sort of mythology of its own. There was tremendous pressure for the 'Second Front', and pupils might talk with older people about their memories of this and of the massive build-up of military equipment and personnel that preceded D-Day. The invasion was far from being a walk-over. The fighting on Omaha Beach was very heavy, and nearly wrecked the whole invasion. Once inland the *bocage* fighting was fierce and difficult. It is worth getting the pupils to plan the equipment they would need to take over with them for a week's fighting as part of the Normandy beachhead, to give them an idea of the logistical problems the Allied planners had to overcome. As well as things like food and ammunition, their list should include how to carry heavy equipment up a sandy beach while under fire (they might try something similar wearing a heavily loaded rucksack) and how to guard against the weather.

The emphasis on D-Day should not exclude consideration of the Russian drive for Berlin. Montgomery wanted to race the Russians to Berlin, but the Americans were happy to let the Russians get there first. Pupils might consider the implications of this for the post-war situation.

Useful reading:
John Keegan's *Six Armies in Normandy* (Penguin) is an excellent account of the complexities of the D-Day campaign. The Overlord Tapestry in Portsmouth is an impressive, though one-sided, portrayal of the campaign marrying the idea of the Bayeux tapestry to the images given in photographs of the campaign. Hugh Trevor-Roper's *The Last Days of Hitler* (Macmillan) remains the best account of Hitler's end in the bunker, based on interviews with survivors just after the fall of Berlin.

The atom bomb (Unit 13)

The arguments about Truman's decision to drop the bomb show no sign of abating. The text here sums up the main considerations as they appeared in 1945. It is very important to consider Truman's dilemma in terms of the context in which he faced it. The choices facing him were more or less as described in the text. There was a proposal that the Japanese should be invited to a demonstration test of the bomb as an alternative to dropping it on a city, though there were doubts expressed about whether or not this would work, and there was always the danger of the bomb not working. Pupils might consider this and other alternatives to the decision to drop the bomb. The decision to drop the second bomb – thereby exhausting the American stock of atomic bombs – needs careful consideration, with a careful look at the chronology in the activities in Resource Sheet Q. Pupils might compare the cases of the Holocaust and Hiroshima: in what ways are they similar, and what differences are there between the two cases?

Useful reading:
Apart from the relevant sections of GCSE texts, there is little available on atomic bombs that is suitable for a young readership, though there are two good passages in the *Faber Book of Reportage* (Faber). For the debate surrounding the dropping of the Bomb see Ronald Spector *Eagle Against the Sun* (Penguin).

Rebuilding Europe (Unit 14)
A Third World War? (Unit 15)
Conclusions

This section is not so much the end as the start of a new era. It is, of course, an era shaped by the war and which, to a great extent, cannot shake off the effects of the war. Pupils might consider the whole question of war crimes, perhaps using exercises in this book, with particular consideration of the issue of continuing to pursue and prosecute Nazi war criminals to this day. They might also consider the question of why there have been no war crimes trials in any of the many wars since 1945, despite frequent threats to set them up. Consideration might be given to the wars in Vietnam, the Middle East and former Yugoslavia.

It is not possible in the pupils' book to go into full detail about the Cold War, which properly demands a book of its own, but pupils might compare the role of the United Nations in the 1940s with its role today. In particular, the way it was born out of the Second World War still has an effect today, notably in the composition of the Security Council. Does this still make sense in the 1990s?

Officially, the Second World War did not end until a final settlement was signed between the wartime allies and the newly reunited Germany in 1990. Pupils might consider the legacy of the war in Europe, particularly the division of Germany and its spectacular reunification in 1989–90. But how many of the problems of the new Germany reflect the problems of the old Germany? In particular, does the re-emergence of violent racism and of neo-Nazi movements suggest that we still have not learnt the lessons of 1939–45?

Useful reading:
A highly readable account of the Nuremberg Trial is given in *Nuremberg* (Coronet) by the escaped POW Airey Neave, who actually served the defendants with their indictments. The situation facing post-war Britain is neatly summed up for children by W.K. Ritchie in *Britain in the Post-War Years, 1945–1951** (Longman Then and There series). Derek Heater's *The Cold War** (Wayland) gives a good introduction to the post-war world for pupils.

Appeasement

Was Chamberlain right to appease Hitler? Could you have done any better? Look at the map and the table, read the memoranda to the Prime Minister, and then write your own memorandum on appeasement.

① Danzig Corridor
② Sudetenland

Source A — Armed forces in 1938

	Great Britain	France	Germany
Army divisions	2	60	80
Fighter aircraft (max. range: 200 km)	406	300	600
Bombers (max. range: 2000 km)	504	450	1600
Battleships	12	7	5
Aircraft carriers	5	1	0
Destroyers (lighter than battleships, but can destroy submarines)	140	70	30
Submarines	50	80	50

History File: Twentieth Century World History, BBC, 1986
Chronicle of the Second World War, Longman, 1990

MEMORANDUM

To: The Prime Minister
From: Mr Winston Churchill, M.P.
Subject: Appeasement

1 Appeasement is madness. We are standing by while Hitler takes over innocent people like the Austrians, the Czechs and now the Poles. We must stand and fight him.

2 Hitler cannot be trusted. It is a waste of time to think he can.

3 We are not as weak as we like to think. We have more fighter planes, and our fleet is much bigger than Germany's. Even if we cannot help places like Austria and the Sudetenland directly, we could always attack Germany itself.

MEMORANDUM

To: The Prime Minister
From: The Foreign Secretary
Subject: Appeasement

1 We are right to appease Hitler. We are not strong enough to stand up to him. He has more men and more aircraft than we and the French have together.

2 The areas he wants to take are too far away for us to do anything to help. The best we can do is to play for time and try and build up our armed forces as quickly as we can.

MEMORANDUM

To: The Prime Minister
From: (Your name)
Subject: Appeasement

From *The Second World War Teacher's Resource Book* © Cambridge University Press 1993

Civil defence

How well would you have done in preparing for bombing? In 1940 people were responsible for whole villages or towns. Imagine you are the Head of the school you are at now, and that you have to make sure your school is safe.

Work in small groups.

Air raid!
You have probably taken part in a fire drill at school. Now you have to work out a similar drill for an air raid.

You will need:
a map of your school
some help from your teacher (in the 'Find out' part)

Make your plan, including

- An estimate of how many air raid shelters you will need, and of what sort (small Anderson shelters, or something larger and more solid?)
- Clear indications of where you will place your air raid shelters
- How you will prevent people panicking or being crushed
- How you will check that everyone is accounted for when you get to the shelters
- What you will do if the Germans drop gas
- What you will do if the school catches fire (remember that it will probably not be the only fire in the area, so the fire brigade may not get to you for some time)
- How you will protect people from falling stonework or tiles

Find out

- How many pupils there are in your school
- How many teachers
- How many non-teaching staff (secretaries, maintenance staff, catering staff, etc)
- Does the school have any large sheltered areas, preferably underground, that could accommodate large numbers of people in safety? If yes, how many people could shelter there?

Remember

- Some areas in your school, such as science laboratories or art rooms, contain a lot of highly inflammable material. Bear this in mind at all times.
- If *anyone* in your school is killed through anything other than enemy action, YOU will be held responsible!

From *The Second World War Teacher's Resource Book* © Cambridge University Press 1993

The Battle of Britain

One of the main reasons why the RAF won the Battle of Britain was because it was well organised.

RAF fighters were carefully guided from the ground so that they made direct contact with the Luftwaffe.

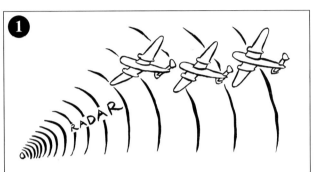

1 When German aircraft took off from their bases in France, they were picked up by high-level RADAR (*RA*dio *D*etection *A*nd *R*anging) Stations, who reported to RAF Fighter Command at Bletchley Park, Stanmore.

2 At Fighter Command the German numbers and direction were carefully logged on a large map of the whole South of England which was divided into three sectors or groups.

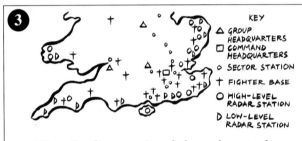

KEY
△ GROUP HEADQUARTERS
□ COMMAND HEADQUARTERS
○ SECTOR STATION
† FIGHTER BASE
O HIGH-LEVEL RADAR STATION
D LOW-LEVEL RADAR STATION

3 When the German aircraft drew closer to the English coast, they were picked up by low-level RADAR Stations and the volunteer Observer Corps who all reported what they picked up to RAF Fighter Command and Group Headquarters who then contacted the nearest Sector Station.

4 At the Sector Station the Germans' progress was logged on a large scale map of the local area. When they were close enough, the Sector Station would telephone the fighter airfields.

5 From the airfields the pilots would 'scramble' to their planes and take off. Once airborne, they would be guided to the target over the radio by the Sector Station, who were still logging the Germans' progress, and could tell the pilots if the Germans changed course.

From *The Second World War Teacher's Resource Book* © Cambridge University Press 1993

The Battle of Britain

Work in groups with half of the group representing the Luftwaffe Commander, Hermann Goering, and his advisers, and the other half representing Air Chief Marshal Hugh Dowding, in charge of Fighter Command, and his staff.

RAF

Look carefully at the Fighter Command Structure to see if you can spot any weak links in it. Try to work out how the Germans could best attack it, and then work out the best way to stop them. You must decide which **two** of these you must defend at all costs (and therefore which ones you might have to leave unprotected):

- RAF airfields
- aircraft factories
- RADAR stations
- Fighter Command Headquarters
- Sector Stations

You must also decide which it is more important to attack:

- German fighters?
- German bombers?

Explain all your choices as carefully as you can.

LUFTWAFFE

Look carefully at the Fighter Command Structure to see if you can spot any weak links in it. Hitler wants you to win quickly. Which **one** of these should you attack most heavily in order to win the battle **fast**?:

- RAF airfields
- aircraft factories
- RADAR stations
- Fighter Command HQ
- Sector Stations

Explain your choice as carefully as you can.

When both groups have finished, compare notes. Using *your* tactics, who would have won the battle?

In reality the Germans began by attacking RAF airfields and RADAR stations. Although the RAF were able to shoot down large numbers of German planes, these attacks were crippling Fighter Command. It was only when the Luftwaffe switched to bombing London and other cities that Fighter Command was able to recover. Would *your* tactics have produced a different result?

From *The Second World War Teacher's Resource Book* © Cambridge University Press 1993

The King of Denmark and the Star of David?

In 1943 the Germans ordered all Danish Jews to wear a yellow armband with a Jewish symbol, the Star of David, on it.

Source A

An American school book tells us what happened :

> The day after the Germans issued the order, seventy-year-old King Christian X of Denmark left his palace wearing a Star of David on his arm. Soon practically every man, woman, and child in Copenhagen defiantly wore a Star of David. The Germans could not arrest them all, and the order was dropped.

R. Conrad Stein, *Resistance Movements*, 1982.

Source B

We find the same story in a novel:

> From German occupation headquarters … came the decree: ALL JEWS MUST WEAR A YELLOW ARM BAND WITH A STAR OF DAVID.
>
> That night the underground [resistance] radio transmitted a message to all Danes: 'King Christian has given the following answer to the German command. He himself will wear the first Star of David and he expects that every loyal Dane will do the same.'
>
> The next day in Copenhagen almost the entire population wore arm bands showing a Star of David.

Leon Uris, *Exodus*, 1990.

Source C

An American historian is not so sure:

> King Christian X … never wore the armband, never even said he would wear it … The Germans never attempted or even threatened to introduce the yellow Star of David in Denmark. … The stories are apocryphal [untrue], but they are an indication of what the Danish people *wanted* to believe about their king.

Harold Flender, *Rescue in Denmark*, 1964.

Source D

Where did the story come from? An Israeli historian has some ideas:

> Already [during the war] the myth was born that the yellow star was not introduced in Denmark because the king was said to have threatened to wear it himself … The fact that in Denmark the Jews were never forced to wear the yellow star … was clearly amazing for people and therefore they tried to find an unusual explanation for it.

Quoted in Leni Yahil, *A Democracy on Trial*, 1967.

Source E

A Danish historian included the story in a book about the German occupation. When he was asked where he got the story he replied:

> I regret to be unable to give you the source of the story about King Christian and the yellow Star of David. I don't think that there actually is any source. The story was on everybody's lips in October 1943.

Quoted in Leni Yahil, *A Democracy on Trial*, 1967.

1 Make two lists, one of sources that believe the story and one of sources that do not.

2 Which of the following statements can we be sure is *true*?

◆ The Germans usually made Jews wear a yellow armband in the countries they conquered.

◆ No one in Denmark wore a yellow armband.

◆ For a long time no one challenged the story.

◆ The Germans were afraid of the Danes.

◆ King Christian was very popular with the Danes.

◆ The Danes still like to think the story is true.

◆ The story is entirely false.

◆ The story is entirely true.

3 Complete the following sentences (think carefully!):

    a If the story is *true*, it shows …

    b If the story is *not* true, it shows …

The Russian Front

The story of the struggle between Hitler and Stalin is told in the boxes below. The order has been jumbled. Read each box and find out:

● When the event happened

● Whether it was to the advantage of Germany or Russia.

Cut out each box and stick it on the right place on Resource Sheet G.

The German forces at Stalingrad surrender.

Stalin goes to war against Finland. The small Finnish army does well against the huge Russian army.

Hitler launches a surprise attack on the USSR.

The German forces reach the outskirts of Moscow.

Hitler and Stalin agree not to attack each other.

Stalin starts to get rid of many of his top officers.

As Russian forces take control of Berlin, Hitler kills himself.

The Russians begin to fight back.

From *The Second World War Teacher's Resource Book* © Cambridge University Press 1993

The Russian Front

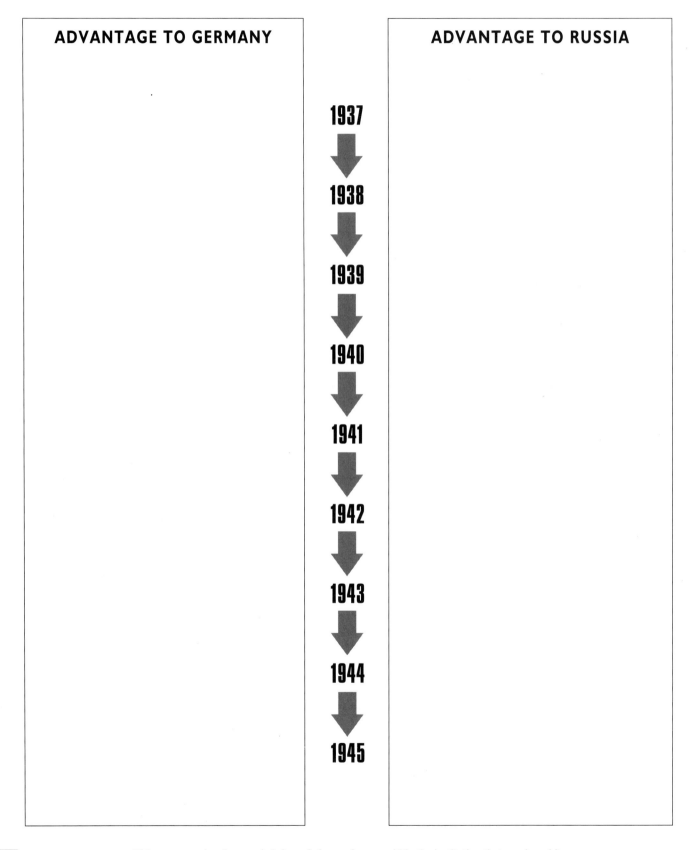

ADVANTAGE TO GERMANY

ADVANTAGE TO RUSSIA

1937

1938

1939

1940

1941

1942

1943

1944

1945

From *The Second World War Teacher's Resource Book* © Cambridge University Press 1993

Pearl Harbor

The Japanese attack on Pearl Harbor brought the USA into the war. It seemed like a great Allied defeat, but was it really? Surprisingly, Winston Churchill said that when he heard the news, he was so pleased that he enjoyed his best night's sleep of the war.

To work out how it is best to view Pearl Harbor, fill in the following boxes. You will need to look through all of the pupils' book to find your evidence.

Take each *theatre* of the war in turn and look up what was happening there in each of the years 1942–1945. Then list the events either as 'Allied Wins' or 'Axis Wins'. (Axis = Germans, Italians, Japanese and their allies.) When you have done that, answer the questions at the bottom of the page.

Theatre of War	Allied Wins	Axis Wins
North Africa (Unit 4)		
Russia (Units 7, 11)		
Atlantic (Unit 4)		
Bombing (Unit 10)		
Italy (Unit 11)		
Pacific and Asia (The war in the east)		
Western Europe (Unit 11)		

Now decide:

1 Where did the USA's entry into the war make
◆ an immediate difference?
◆ a difference in the end?
◆ no difference?

2 Do you think the Japanese attack on Pearl Harbor was:
◆ a gamble that nearly worked
◆ a disaster for the Japanese
◆ a triumph for the Japanese

Explain your reasons carefully.

The Holocaust

Imagine that the war has just finished. Work as a small group. You are British and American lawyers. The Allies have decided to put the leading Nazis who are still alive on trial for 'crimes against humanity'. Your job is to research evidence about the treatment of the Jews. Look at Unit 9 of the pupils' book to find relevant information and write it in the following boxes:

Hitler's views on the Jews

Nazi treatment of the Jews

The ghettos

The death camps

From *The Second World War Teacher's Resource Book* © Cambridge University Press 1993

Code breaking

Could you be a code breaker? You don't just have to be able to solve puzzles: you need to be able to solve them fast, *while the message is still valuable*.

In January 1941 this was found written in a notebook inside a German aeroplane that was shot down near Eastleigh in Hampshire:

Loge	244	142
Schmalstigel	454	149
Bruder	372	120
Suden	272	117
Bild	405	137
		Rückflug

Loge was the German codename for London. *Rückflug* is the German for 'return flight'. The other words are codewords for British cities. You have to work out which ones.

You will need:

♦ a ruler

♦ a pair of compasses

♦ a protractor

The boffins have worked out the figures as follows:

Objective	Distance from base	Compass bearing *to* base
London	244 km	142
Schmalstigel	454 km	149
Bruder	372 km	120
Suden	272 km	117
Bild	405 km	137
	Return Flight	

Now work out:

1 With your compass draw the circle that the German base must lie on (take the distance from London as your radius).

2 Using the compass bearing *from* London, work out where on the circle the base must have been.

3 Using the distances and the compass bearings *to* the base, work out the identities of the other coded towns.

And, since speed is essential, you have to have it all done in **ten** minutes. Get cracking!

RESOURCE SHEET J

From *The Second World War Teacher's Resource Book* © Cambridge University Press 1993

Propaganda

One of the Nazi leaders, Dr Joseph Goebbels, was in charge of German propaganda. That meant it was his job to control all the news reports, radio programmes, books and films that appeared in Germany during the war.

Goebbels was extremely good at his job. He realised that, while people often won't believe little lies, they will always fall for a *big* lie, as long as you repeat it over and over again. These were his rules for successful propaganda:

Propaganda:
♦ must contain just enough truth for people to believe it.
♦ should be repeated often, and loudly.
♦ should play on people's fears, but it should also show them a simple way out.
♦ should come from a source people trust.

Now try using these rules to produce some propaganda of your own. Work in pairs. One of you works for the Allies, and one for the Axis (German, Italian, Japanese) powers. You must each produce either a poster or a short radio announcement about the following events:

Posters:
The Fall of France, 1940
The danger of enemy spies
The Siege of Leningrad
Hiroshima

Radio announcements:
Operation Barbarossa
Pearl Harbor
D-Day
The Battle of the Bulge

When you have done that, compare what you have produced. Have either of you said anything that is not *true*? How did you *use* the events to push forward your point of view?

A FEW CARELESS WORDS MAY END IN THIS—

FOR DANMARK! MOD BOLCHEVISMEN!

From *The Second World War Teacher's Resource Book* © Cambridge University Press 1993

Propaganda

1 You have to explain what is happening in the war to young children. What might be the best ways of doing this? Talk about it first, and then try to do it in a form suitable for 6–7-year-olds. (Remember you must explain it to them but *not* frighten them.)

2 Photographs are an important form of propaganda, but so are the captions to go with them. Choose three photographs in your book, and write suitable captions either for Axis or for Allied propaganda. When you have done that, try and write a *different* caption for the other side.

3 You have to design a leaflet which will be dropped onto enemy troops to persuade them to change sides, or at least to stop fighting. To work, it must be good enough to be taken seriously; it must also have at least some truth in it, otherwise the men will just tear it up. Think very carefully about how you portray your own side in your leaflet: don't forget that the enemy has been reading a lot of propaganda about *you*! Before you put the finishing touches to your leaflet look at what you have written. How would *you* react if you saw it?

From *The Second World War Teacher's Resource Book* © Cambridge University Press 1993

'Funny' Tanks

When the Allies were planning the attack on the Normandy beaches, they had to work out how to overcome the German defences. The British worked out various ingenious ways to use tanks in order to overcome the obstacles they would face in Normandy. See if you can identify the designs which helped the invasion in 1944.

Look at tank design **A** shown below. The tank has been modified into a bulldozer to clear away burnt-out tanks and other heavy vehicles. Now see if you can match tanks **B**, **C**, **D** and **E** with the problems they were designed to solve. These problems are given in the next column.

Try to think of one other problem which the Allies might have faced when they landed in Normandy. Create a new tank design which solves this problem. Describe the problem and draw your solution in frame **F**. (The basic tank has already been drawn. You can add whatever you like to the tank but the only part you can remove is the gun.)

Deep water

It was not always possible for landing craft to come in close enough to land tanks directly onto the beach, especially if the Germans had placed anti-landing craft obstacles on the beach. How can the tank make it from the landing craft to the shore?

Boggy ground

The beach is too soft in parts for heavy vehicles to cross it without sinking in. How can your tank forge a firm path through the sand?

Anti-tank ditch

The ditch is too wide for tanks to cross it, and too deep for them to crawl their way out. How can the tank be used to bridge it *and allow other tanks to cross it as well*?

Minefield

There is no time to seek out each mine individually. How can the tank create a safe path through the minefield *without* blowing up?

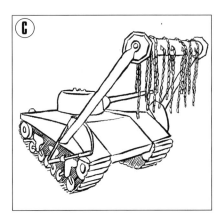

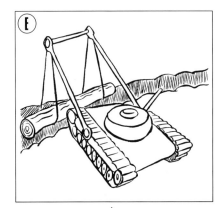

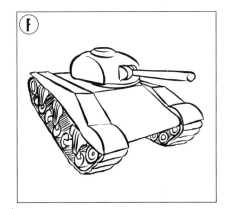

This page may be photocopied, free of charge, for use within the institution that purchased it.

From *The Second World War Teacher's Resource Book* © Cambridge University Press 1993

The Liberation of Paris

As the Allies advanced across France after the D-Day landings in Normandy, Hitler gave special orders for Paris: if the city could not be defended, it was to be destroyed – completely.

The new German Commandant of Paris in 1944 was General von Choltitz. He was a tough, professional soldier who obeyed orders. If he did not, he knew that he would be shot and replaced by someone else who would. He hated the idea of having to destroy Paris, but he was quite used to following orders even if he did not like them.

In this exercise, you are one of General von Choltitz's advisers. On this and the next sheet are some messages he received in August 1944. Read them carefully. It is your job to write underneath each message a suggestion as to how the General should respond. Should he take it seriously? Should he reply at all? And if so, what sort of thing should he say?

GERMAN FORCES GREATER PARIS

From: Colonel Hans Jay
To: Commandant General von Choltitz
Subject: Resistance uprising in Paris

The situation in the streets is extremely serious. Resistance fighters have risen up all over Paris. I have shown the situation on the map below. The rebels are led by the Paris police, who are holding out in the Paris Police Headquarters. So far, my men are keeping things under control: we have retaken some buildings and captured some of the Resistance, but it is a difficult battle and is costing us a lot of men. We *must* have reinforcements.

1 Have I got your permission to start using tanks and high explosives to blow up the buildings the rebels are holding?

2 If nearby buildings are damaged or destroyed, *including some of the famous landmarks of Paris,* will you accept responsibility for this later?

3 Can you persuade Headquarters in Berlin to send us reinforcements?

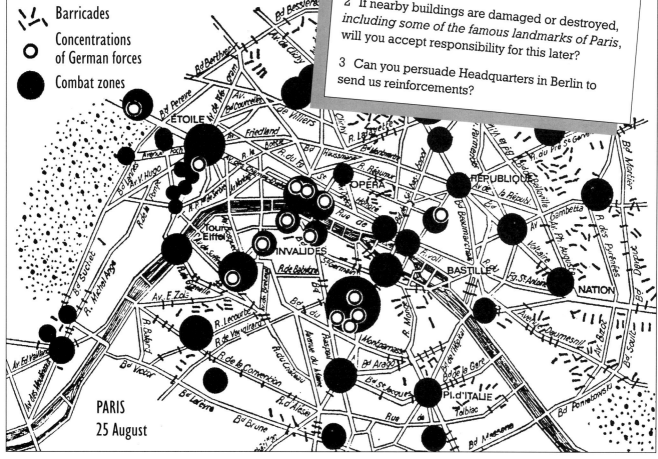

Barricades

Concentrations of German forces

Combat zones

PARIS
25 August

From *The Second World War Teacher's Resource Book* © Cambridge University Press 1993

The Liberation of Paris

ARMY GENERAL HEADQUARTERS BERLIN

From: Field Marshal Jodl

To: General von Choltitz, Commandant of Greater Paris

I regret to inform you that the situation on the eastern front, in France and in Italy will not allow me to spare any troops for the reinforcement of Paris. Good luck!

GERMAN FORCES GREATER PARIS

From: Captain Werner Ebernach, Head of Engineers

To: Commandant General von Choltitz

Subject: Destruction of Paris

Following your orders, my men have now placed explosives and wired them at a number of important points in Paris, including most of the bridges, and famous landmarks like the Eiffel Tower, the Arc de Triomphe, Napoleon's tomb at the Invalides, and the Cathedrals of Sacré-Coeur and Notre-Dame.

However, our supplies are running low and we have not been able to place explosives in nearly enough important buildings like factories, electricity generating plants, railway depots and reservoirs. Colonel Jay has asked me for explosives to use against the Resistance.

1 Should I dismantle explosives on the famous landmarks and move them to factories and power stations, or should I leave them where they are?

2 Can you spare troops to protect my men from attack while they are moving or setting the explosives?

3 Should I send explosives to Colonel Jay?

4 Should I start blowing up the famous Paris monuments and buildings?

EMBASSY OF THE KINGDOM OF SWEDEN PARIS

From: His Excellency the Swedish Ambassador

To: General von Choltitz

I appeal to you in the name of humanity to allow at least a pause in the fighting. If you will allow it, I could help you to arrange a ceasefire when both sides could arrange for the wounded to receive medical attention. This would allow you to postpone the dreadful moment when you have to start destroying the historic buildings of Paris.

REICHSCHANCELLERY BERLIN

From: The Führer

To: General von Choltitz, Commandant of Greater Paris

1 What progress has been made in destroying Paris?

2 Why have I not heard news of the destruction of any important buildings?

3 Why has the Resistance not been destroyed?

From *The Second World War Teacher's Resource Book* © Cambridge University Press 1993

Is Hitler dead?

After the war, many leading Nazis fled to South America. For many years there were rumours that Hitler had escaped from his Berlin bunker to South America too. The Russians captured Berlin in 1945. What did they say happened to Hitler?

Look at the evidence carefully and make up your own mind.

Source A

Marshal Stalin replied that in his opinion Hitler was not dead, but hiding somewhere ... He said that he thought that Goebbels and Hitler had escaped and were in hiding ... It was possible that Hitler and his followers had gone in submarines to Japan.

May 1945 in *The White House Papers of Harry L. Hopkins*.

Source B

Ivan Klimenko was a Russian officer who helped capture Hitler's bunker in Berlin in 1945. In 1979 he recalled:

We started to dig and pulled from the crater the bodies of a man and a woman and two dogs. Of course, I didn't even think that these might be the corpses of Adolf Hitler and Eva Braun since I believed that Hitler's body was already in the Chancellery and only needed to be positively identified.

Source C

A British officer, Hugh Trevor-Roper, was sent into Berlin to talk with people who had been in the bunker with Hitler. Artur Axmann told him in 1946:

As we entered, we saw the Führer sitting on a small sofa, Eva Braun at his side, with her head resting on his shoulder. The Führer was only slightly slumped forward and everyone recognised that he was dead. His jaw hung somewhat loosely down and a pistol lay on the floor. Blood was dripping from both temples, and his mouth was bloody and smeared, but there was not much blood spattered about.

In May 1945 the Russians got hold of two technicians who had worked with Hitler's dentist. They made each of them draw a sketch of Hitler's teeth from memory and then compared the sketches to the teeth of the body in the bunker. The sketches below are based on the drawings by the two technicians. The drawing on the left was made by the technician who had helped with dental work on Hitler only months before. She identified the dental work on the body in the bunker as being Hitler's.

Source D

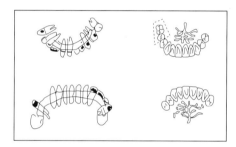

In 1950 Stalin changed his mind and said that not only had the Russians found Hitler's body in the bunker, but that they had shipped it to Moscow. In 1968 the Russians released a photograph which they said showed Hitler's corpse before it was burnt. It showed his face with a bullet wound in the middle of his forehead. His face was otherwise undamaged, and the eyes and mouth were closed as if he were asleep.

RESOURCE SHEET P

From *The Second World War Teacher's Resource Book* © Cambridge University Press 1993

Is Hitler dead?

Source E

HITLER IS ALIVE !

Headline in the *Police Gazette*, January 1977.

Source F

A skull believed to be that of Adolf Hitler has been found in a cardboard box in a Russian archive … Journalist Ella Maximova said she had found it in a cardboard box, together with bloodstained fragments from a sofa.

Daily Express, 19 February 1993.

Source G

Hitler, Adolf (1889–1945). Born at Braunau-on-the-Inn, Upper Austria. At the end of the war, Hitler was cornered in the ruins of Berlin where, as the Russians approached, he married his companion, Eva Braun, and entered into a suicide pact with her, shooting himself on 30 April 1945.

Alan Palmer, *The Penguin Dictionary of Modern History*, 1992.

1 If the *Police Gazette* was right, how old would Hitler have been when the headline was written?

2 Before he found the bodies, what did Ivan Klimenko think had happened to Hitler?

3 Which pieces of evidence would Stalin have known of in 1945 when he spoke to Harry Hopkins (Source A)? Does that evidence suggest he was telling the truth or lying?

4 Look very carefully at the dental drawings in Source D.
◆ In what ways are they similar?
◆ In what ways are they different?
◆ Which drawing is likely to be the more accurate?
◆ Could these sketches be used now to find out what happened to Hitler?
◆ Do you think the jaw found in the Russian archive (Source F) was Hitler's? Give very precise reasons.

5 There is an important difference between Artur Axmann's evidence in Source C and the description of the photograph of Hitler's corpse.
◆ What is it?
◆ Is it an important difference?

◆ Which description do you think is likely to be more accurate?

◆ Could one of these sources be false? Could they both be true? Think carefully.

6 What evidence can you find to support the report in the *Daily Express*?
   If the *Daily Express* report is true, which of these does it *prove*?
◆ Hitler shot himself
◆ Hitler died in 1945
◆ One of the bodies in the bunker was definitely Hitler's
◆ The Russians moved Hitler's body to Moscow

7 What reasons can you think of why newspapers like the *Police Gazette* (and many others) should continue to claim that Hitler is alive?

8 Why do you think the Russians should have pretended for so long not to know what happened?

From *The Second World War Teacher's Resource Book* © Cambridge University Press 1993

Dropping the bomb

Would the Japanese have surrendered even if the Americans had not used their atomic bombs? Look at this chronology carefully and then try to answer the questions at the bottom. If you do not think you have enough evidence to answer a question, leave it blank. Try to find out more information yourself, and then come back to it.

MAY 1945

12 Japanese *kamikaze* suicide pilots attack American Pacific fleet. These raids get more serious as the month goes on.

14 Nagoya, Japan's main aircraft-building city, is flattened by American bombers.

JUNE 1945

21 After three months of bitter fighting, Japanese surrender on Okinawa. The battle cost the Americans 50,000 men. Emperor Hirohito asks his ministers to try to negotiate peace.

27 Kamikaze planes kill 373 men on the USS *Bunker Hill*.

29 Truman agrees invasion plan for Japan, involving five million men.

JULY 1945

10 Heavy American bombing near Tokyo.

13 Japan asks Soviet Union to help negotiate peace with the Allies.

26 Allies demand that Japan surrender *unconditionally* or face destruction.

28 Japan refuses to surrender unless the Allies guarantee that the Emperor should remain on the throne after the war.

29 USS *Indianapolis* sunk by Japanese submarine.

AUGUST 1945

2 Nagasaki and Toyama heavily bombed.

3 All Japanese ports mined by Americans. Allies reconquer Burma.

6 Atom bomb dropped on Hiroshima.

8 Heavy bombing raids on Tokyo and other Japanese cities.

9 Soviet Union declares war on Japan. Russian forces sweep into Manchuria. Atom bomb dropped on Nagasaki.

10 Bombing of Japanese cities continues. Japanese cabinet splits: half want to surrender as long as Emperor is protected; half want guarantee that Japan will not be occupied if they surrender. Emperor votes for immediate surrender.

11 Americans reject Japanese offer, because it still demands guarantees about the Emperor.

12 US destroyer sunk by Japanese submarine.

14 US says the Emperor can remain in power after surrender. Japan surrenders.

1 Does the evidence suggest the Japanese had given up by August 1945? Explain your answer carefully.

2 What condition did the Japanese want before surrendering? Why would the Allies not accept it?

3 Why did the Russians join the war against Japan?

4 Explain in your own words how the Japanese government finally decided to surrender.

5 Now write a careful and full answer to this question: Why did Japan surrender? You should mention:

    the atom bombs   unconditional surrender
    the Emperor   food supplies
    bombing   attacks at sea
    the Russian invasion of Manchuria

From *The Second World War Teacher's Resource Book* © Cambridge University Press 1993

War crimes

All war is cruel, but when exactly does it become a crime? Consider the case of Admiral Karl Doenitz, Commander of Germany's fleet of U-boats. In 1946 he was accused of war crimes for having told his U-boat commanders to attack merchant vessels without warning.

Source A

Admiral Doenitz was prosecuted by Sir David Maxwell-Fyfe and defended by Fleet-Advocate Kranzbuhler. This is a transcript of part of his trial:

Kranzbuhler: What were the orders which you received at the beginning of the war for the conduct of the U-boat warfare?

Doenitz: I could attack without warning all ships which were guarded either by naval vessels or which were under air cover. Furthermore, I was permitted to exercise armed force against any ship which when stopped sent radio messages, or resisted the order to stop, or did not obey the order to stop.

Kranzbuhler: What measures did the enemy take?

Doenitz: Right at the beginning of the war it was our experience that all [Allied] merchantmen immediately sent messages as soon as they saw any U-boat on the horizon. It was absolutely clear, therefore, that all merchantmen were co-operating in the military intelligence service. Furthermore, only a few days after the beginning of the war we found out that merchantmen were armed and made use of their weapons.

Maxwell-Fyfe: Do you consider sailing without lights is either persistent refusal to stop or active resistance?

Doenitz: If a merchant ship sails without lights it must run the risk of being taken for a warship, because at night it is not possible to distinguish between a merchant ship and a warship.

Source B

US Admiral Nimitz, Commander of the US Pacific Fleet, made this statement in 1946:

It was customary for U.S. submarines to attack any [Japanese] merchantman without warning.

Work in groups of about five. You will have to decide whether Admiral Doenitz is guilty or not guilty. To do that, answer questions 1, 2 and 3 first.

1 Lieutenant Kranzbuhler wanted to use Source B. As you can see, it is not about Admiral Doenitz, nor even about the U-boat war. Should he be allowed to use it in court?

2 There were *five* types of case when U-boats had orders to attack merchant ships. List what these were. Then decide which of these you think are acceptable in time of war.

3 Why might ships in wartime sail without lights? Do you think Admiral Doenitz is right when he says that they can then be attacked?

4 What is your verdict?

◆ If you think the German U-boats followed the normal rules of war you must vote *Not guilty*

◆ If you think the German U-boats went beyond the normal rules of war you must vote *Guilty*

The Truman Doctrine and Marshall Aid

After the war, the American Secretary of State, General George C. Marshall, drew up a plan for America to pay out huge sums of money to help the European countries to recover from the war. The plan was called the *Marshall Plan*.

At the same time, President Truman came up with a different plan, to send American help to any country that was fighting against communists. His plan was called the *Truman Doctrine*.

The Russians said the Marshall Plan and the Truman Doctrine were linked.

Your task:

One of the countries interested in accepting American help under the Marshall Plan was Czechoslovakia. Look at the following pieces of evidence carefully, and then write a short party political broadcast either *for* or *against* accepting American aid under the Marshall Plan.

Remember that Czechoslovakia is in the Soviet-controlled half of Europe!

Source A

General Marshall describes his plan:

> Our policy is directed not against any country or doctrine, but against hunger, poverty, desperation and chaos.

Quoted in N. Lowe, *Mastering Modern World History*, 1982.

Source B

President Truman describes his doctrine:

> I believe that it must be the policy of the United States to support free people who are resisting attempted take-over by armed minorities or by outside pressures. I believe that help should be primarily through economic and financial aid.

Quoted in P. King, *Modern World Affairs Made Simple*, 1984.

Between 1948 and 1952 Marshall Aid was given to 17 western European countries. They received $13 billion of cash, credit, machinery, food, petrol, coal, steel and cotton.

The first countries to receive aid were Greece and Turkey. Both countries were fighting communist guerrilla groups at the time. American aid helped them to defeat the communists, and both countries quickly became firm American allies.

Source C

This is how Soviet Foreign Minister Molotov described the Marshall Plan:

> Dollar Imperialism ... A cunning attempt to rescue American capitalism by economically enslaving Europe. Marshall Aid means American control.

From *The Second World War Teacher's Resource Book* © Cambridge University Press 1993

End of empire

In the years that followed the end of the war in 1945, the huge empires of Britain and France quickly collapsed. Many of the reasons were connected with the war. Think carefully about all that you have read and learnt, and then look at this list of causes and consequences. Try to put them together. You can put as many causes to each consequence as you like, or as many consequences to each cause. Remember that you must be able to explain your choice.

Causes

(all of these statements are true)

A Britain and France could not afford to defend their huge empires either before the war or after.

B Mahatma Gandhi led a huge but non-violent campaign during the war calling for an independent India.

C There were strong Communist resistance movements which fought against the Japanese in Asia.

D Thousands of Jewish people fled from Nazi Germany to Britain and the USA.

E Indian troops fought bravely against the Germans and Japanese.

F The British were humiliated by the Fall of Singapore in 1942.

G Calling for independence in wartime looked like treason.

H Britain elected a Labour government in 1945.

I World opinion was shocked by the Nazi Holocaust.

J America refused to help keep the European empires going after the war.

K In Palestine after the war Jewish terrorists started attacking British soldiers to force the British to withdraw.

Consequences

(all of these statements are true)

1 The British locked Gandhi up during the war.

2 India did not become independent until after the war.

3 The European empires fell to the Japanese during the war.

4 India became independent in 1947.

5 Britain pulled out of Palestine in 1948.

6 The UN declared the State of Israel in 1948.

7 Many Asian countries did not want the Europeans back after the war.

 From *The Second World War Teacher's Resource Book* © Cambridge University Press 1993

The war remembered

There are many reminders today of the events of the Second World War. You can see memorials to the people who died in the war in almost any town or village. It still provides the setting for films, television programmes, books, news stories, even toys.

Look carefully at these examples of how the memory of the war is still used and answer the questions that follow them.

Source A

This comes from a comic book, like many you can buy in newsagents' shops:

Source B

Exeter Cathedral will be the venue for a special service to commemorate the Exeter blitz on May 3.

The German ambassador to the UK will be attending, along with a civic party from Lübeck, Germany, led by the City President.

The service takes place on the 50th anniversary of the blitz.

The service, which starts at 11 am, will be broadcast live by Television South West.

Express and Echo, 1992

© *Commando* D.C. Thomson & Co., Ltd 1993

1 For each of sources A and B answer the following questions:

♦ Who is this aimed at?

♦ What does it make people think about the war?

♦ What makes you think that?

The war remembered

2 This is an observation assignment. Find one example of each of the following ways of remembering the war. Name each example and write a brief description including who you think it is aimed at and what its effect is on the people who see it.

Memorial	Description
A war memorial	
A war film	
A television or radio documentary programme about the war	
A schoolbook about the war	
A museum or exhibition	
A model kit, game or toy based on the war	
A piece of fiction or poetry dealing with the war	

3 Remembering your previous answers, consider this difficult issue:

Source C

In 1990 the *Times Educational Supplement* (a newspaper for teachers) reported:

> Historian Dr Lionel Kochan argues that the Holocaust should not be taught in schools or colleges at all. Teaching the Holocaust encourages a view of Jewish history dominated by persecution, making a repetition of the Holocaust more likely.

But Dr Ronnie Landau disagreed: 'Do we want our children to find out about the Holocaust from bad movies, from crude jokes …?'

Times Educational Supplement, 7 December 1990.

Who do you think was right? Think carefully about this, and your previous ideas about why and how we remember the events of the Second World War, before giving your answer.

From *The Second World War Teacher's Resource Book* © Cambridge University Press 1993